EVA DI CESARE graduated from Victorian College of the Arts in 1989 and is one of the founding members of Monkey Baa Theatre Company.

Most recently she directed the company's production of Randa Abdel-Fattah's *Where the Streets Had a Name* and Jackie French and Bruce Whatley's *Diary of A Wombat*, which toured to 59 venues throughout Australia and was invited to showcase in Philadelphia, USA, at the International Performing Arts for Youth Conference (IPAY).

Eva co-adapted the Sydney Theatre Award-winning play of Li Cunxin's *The Peasant Prince*, the Helpmann Award-winning plays of Jackie French's *Hitler's Daughter* and Sonya Hartnett's *Thursday's Child*, Tim Winton's *The Bugalugs Bum Thief*, Morris Gleitzman's *Worry Warts*, Gillian Rubinstein's *The Fairy's Wings*, Stephen Michael King's *Milli, Jack and the Dancing Cat*, Susanne Gervay's *I Am Jack*, Elizabeth Fensham's *Goodbye Jamie Boyd*, Duncan Ball's *Emily Eyefinger*, Jackie French and Bruce Whatley's *Pete the Sheep* and Jackie French's *Josephine Wants to Dance*.

Eva's acting credits include *The Bugalugs Bum Thief*, *Worry Warts* and *The Fairy's Wings* for Monkey Baa; the world premiere of *Disarming Rosetta* (Hothouse Theatre 2011), written by Rosalba Clemente and directed by Tom Healey; *Una Festa di Nozze* (Doppio Teatro, Adelaide Festival and Singapore Festival 1996); *Emma* and *Love and Magic in Mamma's Kitchen* (Belvoir St 1995/1991); *Ricordi* (Doppio Teatro and Melbourne Festival 1990); *A Play on Worlds* (Kings Bloody Cross Theatre 1990) and *Five Times Dizzy* (Theatre South 1999). She has also played a leading role and was musical director for Theatre South's *Italian Stories*. Film and TV credits include *All Saints*, *GP*, *A Country Practice*, *Bony*, *Police Rescue*, *English at Work* and *Last Days of Chez Nous*.

In 2013 Eva developed and facilitated the Discover the Stage—Digital Drama Workshops for the Sydney Opera House with Tim McGarry. They also co-wrote and directed the 2013 Opera House Babies Proms Series and *Snugglepot and Cuddlepie* (with Sandra Eldridge) for CDP Theatre Producers and *Simon Tedeschi Pianist and Prankster* for Monkey Baa.

Eva is currently co-writing *Possum Magic*, based on the wonderful picture book by Mem Fox and Julie Vivas.

Aanisa Vylet (left) as Hayaat and Mansoor Noor as Samy in the 2017 Monkey Baa production at Lendlease Darling Quarter Theatre, Sydney. (Photo. Michael Bourchier)

WHERE THE STREETS HAD A NAME

Eva Di Cesare

based on the book by

Randa Abdel-Fattah

CURRENCY PLAYS

First published in 2018
by Currency Press Pty Ltd,
PO Box 2287, Strawberry Hills, NSW, 2012, Australia
enquiries@currency.com.au
www.currency.com.au

Typeset by Dean Nottle for Currency Press.
Printed by Fineline.
Cover design by Alissa Dinallo.

A catalogue record for this book is available from the National Library of Australia

Contents

Mansoor Noor (left) as Samy and Dina Gillespie as Mama in the 2017 Monkey Baa production at Lendlease Darling Quarter Theatre, Sydney. (Photo: Michael Bourchier)

INTRODUCTION

Let me start by telling you about my father and his village. And to do that I must start in 1945.

In this year my father was born in Burqa, in the West Bank of Palestine. The village is breathtakingly beautiful, high in the hills and mountains near the town of Nablus, with a view of the Mediterranean Sea on a clear night. My father's home is a magnificent structure, made of white limestone, with ornate patterns on its doors and windows, and the original mosaic tiles on its floors. It sits on a huge plot of land filled with olive and fruit trees. Eighteen years ago, a limestone verandah wrapped around the front of the house, and my sister and I stood on it with my parents, attempting to carefully extract my father's school certificate from an old photo frame—a part of his childhood that he had to leave behind. The stones of the verandah have since collapsed, and the house is in ruins.

Burqa has been under Israeli military occupation since 1967 and none of my father's family has been allowed to return to live in the house and, therefore, look after it. Most of the people my father knew and grew up with are in exile or dead, or else living as second-class citizens in Jordan. My own extended family are in Jordan but denied the right to live in their homeland. My father was permitted to return in 2000 only as an 'Australian tourist'. On our arrival at the Sheikh Hussein Bridge between Jordan and occupied Palestine, a young, cocky soldier wagged his finger at my father and warned him that he was visiting a Jewish state. 'Adnan,' he said, 'I will let you stay for seven days only'. It was not lost on me that this 'boy' wasn't even born when my father was exiled from his land.

My father was three years old when the state of Israel was declared. This had a devastating and continuing impact on my father's family. In 1967 my father became officially stateless and dispossessed of the right to return to his birthplace. He was awarded a UN refugee scholarship to study in Egypt and eventually ended up on a scholarship to do his PhD in Australia, which has been his home since 1973. Despite the existence of our ancestral home in Burqa, my relatives are all in Jordan, either in the predominantly refugee suburb of Zarqa, or Amman. They have been dying off there, buried in a country to which they do not belong, deprived of the right to even touch the soil of their homeland before they died. Visiting my father's homeland for the first time in 2000, when I was a university student, was life-changing. It had been thirty-five years since my father had seen his homeland. Thirty-five years since he'd travelled through its hills and mountains; talked and mixed with his people; wrapped his arms around its olive and fruit trees; eaten the food he had grown up on. Burqa, his village, had never stopped calling him, beckoning him to return to his land, to make the journey from Australia back to the home he was born in.

Until I visited, Burqa had always been like a fantasy-land to me, a Palestinian Narnia of my father's past. I had seen no photographs, so my imagination ran wild with its description. As soon as we crossed from Jordan into Palestine, I was overwhelmed to discover that here a person's roots mattered. From the hotel concierge in Jerusalem, to the tour guide at the Nativity Church in Bethlehem, to the people who sat beside us in the buses we rode, everybody here understood that there is dignity in being able to claim heritage, in being able to trace identity, lineage, story from an olive tree, a rocky hill, a winding mountain road. I soaked it all up. I felt a connection to this place that was so visceral, so instinctive, that it ached. The injustice of dispossession, ethnic cleansing and occupation filled us with rage. I remember sitting on a minibus at a checkpoint near Bethlehem, watching two soldiers humiliate a family wanting to board. After insulting and ridiculing them, and clearly having fun doing it, the family embarked. My parents, sister and I later marvelled at the forbearance of the locals in such an utterly dehumanising and shocking situation.

When I returned with my father and daughter (who was five at the time), for our second and last visit to Palestine six years ago, things were worse. A massive, monstrous concrete wall illegally snaked its way through the West Bank. Bethlehem, for example, was now completely sealed within it. In Australia, access to some roads depends on e-tags. In Israel, road access is racially determined. Driving on roads reserved for Israelis only, built on land confiscated from Palestinians—some of whom I met and who showed me the title deeds to their land—I noted the wide lanes, line markings and lighting. The roads for Palestinians were disgraceful, winding through high hills and mountains with no bitumen, line markings, lanes or lights. It was like driving blindfolded on the road to the Blue Mountains! I saw Israeli 'settlers' swagger about at bus shelters, guns on display, as Palestinians stood several metres away, dutifully maintaining their place. I watched Palestinians herded into metal cages at Qalandiya Checkpoint, between the West Bank and Jerusalem, ordered about, often in the broken Arabic the soldiers have learned, although the swear words were always coherent. I met a man whose vineyard had been seized by settlers and was now compelled to work as an employee on his own land.

On both my visits to Palestine, I was overcome by many things, but one thing stood out for me: the determination of people to try to make an ordinary life for themselves in extraordinary circumstances. I can't forget the image of a weary-eyed mother scolding her children, who were pinching each other, as we waited at a checkpoint. Even surrounded by the insanity of soldiers wielding AK47s as they order people around, kids will be kids. When I travelled through Palestine, I was intrigued by the way the macro-politics of the country infiltrated the everyday spaces of people's lives. The human condition, people's needs and wants, are basically the same. You don't get to opt out of bickering siblings, marital strain, 'frenemies' at school, toddler tantrums, depression, falling into giddy heights of love, diva brides or gossiping neighbours just because you're living under a brutal military occupation. Life has to go on. And it does, sometimes to tragic, sometimes to comic, effect.

This is why I wrote *Where the Streets Had a Name*. I wanted my readers to understand what Palestinians are up against. To appreciate the resilience, courage and determination it takes to insist on a life worth living, even when everything is stacked against you. And I especially wanted my readers to understand this from the point of view of young people.

The first time I saw Israel's grey, cement wall on Monkey Baa's stage, I cried. I cried during rehearsals, I cried on opening nights at Riverside Theatre and Darling Quarter. I cried when I heard young students from Western Sydney recount their own family's histories and stories on the stage. I cried when my father cried during the play. I cried when some of my family's oldest Palestinian friends attended with their large families and thanked us for bringing a touch of Palestine to Sydney. I cried a lot, but they were always, always tears of indescribable joy. Monkey Baa Theatre Company, who believed in this story and made it possible, Eva Di Cesare, who wrote the script, the incredible actors who each brought something of their own stories to their characters and shone on stage, the creative and production team— they all gave me the most precious gift a writer can dream of: the privilege of seeing one's words and story through other people's hearts and minds. I was blessed to have a scriptwriter like Eva. She worked so hard to really understand my story and my father's story. Even before she put pen to paper, she met with us both and listened to my father tell her his life story over lunch and coffee. I was privileged to witness this. I heard him share stories I'd never heard before. With the production of *Where the Streets Had a Name*, I was gifted another side to my father that I had never encountered before.

I don't know if there will ever be anything as magical again in my life as sitting in a theatre and witnessing children and young adults laugh, gasp for breath, click their tongues, lean their tense bodies in close to the stage. Students who watched the play as part of a school excursion spoke to me and the actors afterwards. The mood was one of collective transformation. When one thinks of the ongoing and escalating violence and injustice meted against Palestinians who simply want freedom, one can feel overwhelmed with helplessness. But nothing has been more powerful in proving to me the power of art to make a difference than the experience of my book being adapted to the stage for predominantly school audiences. Theatre is intimate, up close and personal. This play gave audiences the opportunity to meet Palestine. And I still get goosebumps thinking about how privileged and humbled I am to have been a part of that.

At the end of the play, my family hugged me and told me they were proud of me. Everything to do with my writing I do for my family, for the people I love, because that is what the fight for human rights is ultimately about: individual lives. No more unique, deserving or different to our own. Just people, who deserve the same freedom we take for granted. So when an audience sees Hayaat and her family arguing over who has been evicted on 'Arabs Got Talent' during an Israeli-imposed curfew, this play offers people something more real, possibly more comprehensible than any law, declaration or UN resolution. In the end, it is story that connects people. And I hope this script will connect with you.

Randa Abdel-Fattah
June 2018

Randa Abdel-Fattah is a multi-award winning author of eleven books. Her young adult and children's books are published in over fifteen countries.

From left: Alissar Gazal as Sitti Zeynab, Dina Gillespie as Mama and Aanisa Vylet as Hayaat in the 2017 Monkey Baa production at Lendlease Darling Quarter Theatre, Sydney. (Photo: Michael Bourchier)

Where the Streets Had a Name was first produced by Monkey Baa Theatre Company and premiered at Riverside Theatres, Parramatta, on 30 August 2017, with the following cast:

HAYAAT	Aanisa Vylet
SAMY / TARIQ	Mansoor Noor
BABA	Sal Sharah
MAMA	Dina Gillespie
SITTI ZEYNAB	Alissar Gazal

Director, Eva Di Cesare
Assistant Director, Claudia Chidiac
Dramaturg, Tim McGarry
Set and Costume Designer, Antoinette Barbouttis
Lighting Designer, Emma Lockhart-Wilson
Composer / Sound Designer, Oonagh Sherrard
AV Designer, Jerome Pearce
Production and Stage Manager, Cally Bartley
Technical Coordinator, Jeremy Page
Cultural Advisors, Melia Shammas, Hilal Asmar, Reeda Khassis, Sarah Issa Shaweesh, Alham Najar

The play was developed in collaboration with the students of Sir Joseph Banks High School.

CHARACTERS

HAYAAT, 13 years old

MAMA (NUR), Hayaat's mother

BABA (FOAD), Hayaat's father

TARIQ, 9, Hayaat's younger brother

SITTI ZEYNAB, 75, Hayaat's grandmother

SAMY, 13, Hayaat's best friend

WASIM, 13, a refugee from the AIDA refugee camp

MOLLY, Israeli peace activist

JEWISH MAN

JEWISH WOMAN

SIDI, Hayaat's grandfather

AMTO AMAL, passenger on bus to Beit Sahur

ABO AZAM, driver of bus to Beit Sahur

KARIM, driver of bus from Deir Salah

BUS DRIVER, driver of bus to Container Checkpoint

YOSSI, Israeli taxi driver

SOLDIERS

Maysaa, Hayaat's friend who has died, appears only onscreen

SETTING

This play is set in Palestine.

PROLOGUE

We open on an empty moonlit stage, except for a half-built wall upstage. As the action unfolds, we hear a solitary female voice sing.

MAMA *appears and begins to put on her hijab, ready for the day.*

BABA *appears on an elevated platform as if he is on a mountain top looking out over the olive groves down below. He holds papers in his hands.*

SITTI ZEYNAB *appears, sitting in an armchair, holding tightly to a carved wooden box. She opens it and pulls out a photograph.*

HAYAAT *appears downstage. She is performing a ritual ablution. The right side of her face is scarred. She peers into the mirror in front of her and is startled by her reflection. She raises a hand to cover the right part of her face. She slowly lowers her hand and sees a stranger again.*

An image of two girls appears on the wall, dancing the Dabke. They are Hayaat and Maysaa.

SAMY *enters upstage with a paint tin and brush. He begins to paint on the wall.*

The letters appear as a graphic on the wall as he paints.

The wording is 'Fight the wall until it fal …'

As the singing ends …

The sound of a siren signalling the end of curfew.

SCENE ONE: THE GROCERY STORE

2004.

Afternoon.

Loud voices can be heard in a grocery store. We hear the shopkeeper trying to keep order.

The dinging sound of a cash register

*The family enters the store—*MAMA, BABA, HAYAAT, TARIQ. MAMA *takes charge. She hands a bag out to each of her family as she gives them a list. She is highly strung and stressed and everyone is moving too slowly for her liking.*

MAMA: *Yallah!* Wretched curfews! So many people. *Yallah!* We have one hour before we have to be back home. *Yallah!* Move! Foad! Get four packets of soap, shavers, toilet paper …

BABA: How much?

MAMA: What?

BABA: Toilet paper. How much?

MAMA: *Ya rabi!* Four!

BABA: This shop is a mess. Which aisle?

MAMA: Aisle three! Toilet paper, pads, toothpaste, toothbrushes, four of everything! Aisle three. Don't forget! Hayaat! Potatoes, eggs, labne, olives …

HAYAAT: When is this curfew going to end, Mama?

MAMA: Have I got the mind of an Israeli? Ask them. I told you, we have one hour. Keep your eyes open. You're wasting time. Potatoes, eggs, labne, olives, tahini, sugar, flour, salt and rice.

TARIQ: But why are we always in a hurry? What are these curfews for?

MAMA: To control us.

TARIQ: But, Mama …

MAMA: Enough now, Tariq! Go and get the hummus. We are going to be late. Get the hummus. As many jars as you can carry. *Yallah!* I'll get the candles and the batteries. Don't forget a thing!

They all look at her, waiting for any other instructions.

Yallah!

They all run off.

Many people can be heard arguing in the store, pushing to get to the front of the queue.

The family all return, laden with groceries. BABA *comes in first, but he is reluctant to join the queue.*

[*To* BABA] Why aren't you at the cash register? We don't have much time left!

BABA: Look at all these people in the queue. *Majaneen!* We will be trampled and I'm wearing my best suit. I picked it out especially.

MAMA *gives* BABA *a death stare.*

What? You never know who you'll meet when a curfew is lifted.

MAMA: *Ya rabi!* Better to be trampled here than be out on the streets when the curfew is back on! *Majnoun enta hammak ala aweek? Mesh khaif ala halak.* The things he thinks about at a time like this! *Yallah!*

MAMA *pushes her way to the front of the queue. The family look at each other and follow.*

SCENE TWO: CURFEW

Early morning.

At home in the kitchen/lounge room. HAYAAT *is preparing for school.*

MAMA *enters the kitchen.*

MAMA: Good morning, Hayaat.
HAYAAT: Good morning, Mama.
MAMA: Did you sleep well?

HAYAAT *doesn't respond.*

Beat.

Is your brother ready?
HAYAAT: No.
MAMA: Tariq! *Yallah!* You will be late for school!

A siren goes off, signalling that there is a curfew on.

Damn curfews! Again! *Meen bi-fakruh halhom?* [Who do they think they are?] No warning. They only lifted it last night. We will need to ration our supplies. Wipe the crumbs off the bench. You can do your homework first. Then you can help me clean out the kitchen cupboards.
HAYAAT: Baba forgot the toothbrushes.
MAMA: Ooff! I knew it. Use Tariq's old one.

TARIQ *enters and hears this. He and* HAYAAT *both make disgusted sounds.*

TARIQ: No school. Yes! [*To* HAYAAT] You've wet the bed again.
HAYAAT: Shut up.
MAMA: Tariq.
TARIQ: It's disgusting. It stinks. I need my own bed.
MAMA: Tariq, enough!

She gives TARIQ *a look that indicates 'Stop now, or else!'*

BABA *enters with his papers and sits in an armchair with his own thoughts.*

[*To* HAYAAT] Habibti, you are my precious one. May God find you a good husband one day who will ignore this scar and love you for who you are on the inside.

TARIQ: At least you won't have to see Khaled at school today.

MAMA: Who's Khaled?

TARIQ: Khaled is a donkey! He is the poo of a donkey. He is the insect that feeds on the poo of a donkey.

MAMA: Don't use such language!

TARIQ: But he calls Hayaat 'potato mash' face.

MAMA: Enough! Where did you learn this language?

TARIQ: From you, yesterday. You told Khalto Samar that the bathroom smells like poo because—

MAMA: Enough!

TARIQ: But you said—

MAMA: Enough!

SITTI *enters. They run to her to help her.*

SITTI: *Ya Allah!* How can my Hayaat learn when there is so much disruption?

They all help her gently into her chair.

Ya Allah! Ease these bones of mine.

HAYAAT: Do you want to eat some breakfast, Sitti Zeynab?

SITTI: Too early. Maybe later. But you eat! Strength, my darling, you must eat. You're so thin. You must fill your stomach. Otherwise your brain will sleep. How else will you become a doctor? Or was it a dentist? I can never remember which one … Eat!

MAMA: You forgot the toothbrushes, Foad.

HAYAAT: I need a toothbrush, Baba.

SITTI: And I need a hip replacement. Such is life. Leave him alone, Habibti. You can see he's busy.

MAMA: Ouff! Busy!

HAYAAT *hands* SITTI *a cup of coffee.*

SITTI: God reward you and heal your face, Habibti.

Lighting change.

HAYAAT: My face, my face! If I hear one more reference to my face, I'll scream.

An image of Maysaa's face appears on the screen. HAYAAT *feels the presence of Maysaa but ...*

No.

She snaps out of this moment.

[*To the audience*] I want to be back in Beit Jala, before we came here to Bethlehem and our tiny apartment. I don't remember much … My memory is like a patchwork quilt with holes. But I remember our house. I remember climbing the olive trees at sunrise when I was nine. I remember Baba.

SCENE THREE: BABA AND BEIT JALA

2000.

In the olive grove.

Dawn.

BABA *is sitting under an olive tree.* HAYAAT *is in the tree. She is counting all the trees in their olive grove.*

The sun is just about to break.

BABA: Hayaat!
HAYAAT: 85, 86, 87, 88, 89, 90, 91, 92, 93 …
BABA: Come down from there. If your mother sees you, I'll be dead.
HAYAAT: 94, 95, 96, 97 …
BABA: Hayaat, get down.
HAYAAT: 98, 99, 100! We've got a hundred olive trees!

HAYAAT *climbs down from the tree and joins* BABA *under the olive tree.*

BABA: Yes we do. They are holy trees, Hayaat. They've been in our family for many generations. Olive trees are sacred. They're even mentioned in the Quran. Mary, beloved mother of Jesus, peace be upon him, took refuge under an olive tree when the pangs of her labour were too much to bear.
HAYAAT: It was a palm tree, Baba.
BABA: No.

HAYAAT: Yes. It was.

BABA: Are you sure?

HAYAAT: Yes. I learned it at school. She shook the leaves of the palm tree in Bethlehem and ate from the dates.

BABA: Well, palm trees, olive trees, what's the difference? The roots of this land are holy, Hayaat. Oh, and Hayaat?

HAYAAT: Hm?

BABA: Don't tell your teacher.

HAYAAT: Yes, Baba.

BABA *is looking out at the mountains way in the distance.*

BABA: Listen, Hayaat. Listen.

HAYAAT: I can't hear anything. It's quiet.

BABA: Yes. Listen to the quiet. Did you know that the sun asks God's permission to rise and set every day? Here it comes, Hayaat. Look.

Silence.

The lights get a tiny bit brighter as the sun begins to peek over the back of the mountain.

HAYAAT: I can see it, Baba. And I can see Jebal Abo Ghnaim. Who lives there? I think fairies live there.

BABA: Maybe. There are many Christian holy sites on that mountain, Hayaat.

Lighting change.

HAYAAT: [*to the audience*] And then ... it was all gone. Bulldozers trampled through Jebal Abo Ghnaim soon after that and there were no more sunrises with Baba. Why did they come for our land? Why am I here in this cramped two-bedroom apartment, sharing a bed with my little brother and grandmother?

I follow Baba sometimes, to the highest point in Bethlehem, to the lookout which faces Beit Jala. He stands for hours, like a man standing at a headstone in a cemetery.

I don't know what happened to him. What happened to him?

SCENE FOUR: MAMA AND THE VINE LEAVES

2004.

Afternoon.

MAMA *is in the kitchen.*

HAYAAT *enters.*

MAMA: There you are, Hayaat. *Yallah!* Help me finish the *warak dawali.* I don't know what happened to the time. They won't be ready for dinner.

HAYAAT *joins* MAMA *and helps roll the vine leaves.*

How was your father today? Did you follow him?

HAYAAT: Yes.

MAMA: Well, where did he go?

HAYAAT: He … went to the cafe.

MAMA: Who was he with?

HAYAAT: Abo Hussein.

MAMA: That's all? Just to the cafe?

HAYAAT: Yes.

MAMA: All day? Nowhere else.

HAYAAT: Yes. All day.

Beat.

Mama, what happened in Beit Jala?

MAMA: What are you bringing that up for?

HAYAAT: I need to talk about it.

MAMA: I haven't got time to talk about the past, Hayaat.

HAYAAT: Mama, I need to know.

Pause.

Why did you send me away?

MAMA: When?

HAYAAT: In Beit Jala, the day you sent me into town with Sitti. Why did you send me away?

MAMA: Hayaat.

HAYAAT: Mama, I want to know.

Pause.

MAMA: We couldn't let you see. That's enough.
HAYAAT: See what? What did they do?
MAMA: *Halas!*
HAYAAT: Come on, Mama. I need to know. Please.
MAMA: Ah, Hayaat. Habibti. It started two years before that day. We were given an order.
HAYAAT: An order?
MAMA: A confiscation order.
HAYAAT: For what?
MAMA: They were going to take over our home.
HAYAAT: Why? Why would they do that?
MAMA: They needed to make way for a road to connect the Israeli settlements to each other.
HAYAAT: A road?

BABA *enters holding his worry beads and papers.*

MAMA: Yes. A road. Tell her what happened, Foad.
HAYAAT: Baba, tell me what happened in Beit Jala?

BABA *is reluctant to speak.*

MAMA: Tell her what you did when I handed you the confiscation order.

Pause.

Foad, tell her.

Pause.

I gave it to him. He tore it up and we sat down to eat and he refused to speak about it again.
BABA: Nur, enough.
HAYAAT: When did they come?
MAMA: After two years of living in fear … the demolition order came. We had one week to get out. Foad, tell her. She's old enough and after what she's been through herself …
BABA: Tell her what, Nur? Tell her what? That they made me kneel? Pointed their guns at me and laughed? They bulldozed my house, my trees. And I couldn't stop it. Will talking about it change anything, Nur?
HAYAAT: Why did you send me away, Baba? I would have helped you fight.

BABA: Habibti, you were nine years old. What could you have done? You can't fight bulldozers with stones. I couldn't stop it, Habibti. I couldn't stop it.

BABA *is shaking. He exits.*

HAYAAT: Baba.

MAMA: I remember it like it was yesterday. The noise. First they destroyed the water tanks, the ones we used to irrigate the farmland. Then a building your father used to store the equipment.

When they came for our house, I couldn't control myself ... my home ... I ran towards it, but a line of soldiers was barricading the front gate, protecting the bulldozers. I wanted to hit them. I wanted to crush them. I've never felt such rage, Hayaat. Then the walls fell.

HAYAAT: And Baba?

MAMA: The neighbours had to hold him back. They pinned him to the ground as he screamed.

And then ... when they started on the olive trees, that was the most terrible thing of all.

Pause.

HAYAAT: I miss our land, Mama.

MAMA: It's all under concrete now. But we have two choices, Hayaat. We either try to survive or we give up. We can't give up, Hayaat. Never give up.

MAMA *exits with the finished vine leaves.*

HAYAAT: [*to the audience*] I think of the cars that drive on that road now on top of our home and ... I wonder if they know that our lives are buried underneath it.

SCENE FIVE: 'X FACTOR'

2004.

Evening.

The lounge room.

The sound of the UK program 'X Factor' is heard coming from the television.

HAYAAT *and* TARIQ *are finishing homework.*

They're all watching television intently. BABA *remains silent.*

We hear the final line of one female contestant and the audience applause.

SITTI: Oh, thank God she's stopped. What a mouth she has. Too much noise.

HAYAAT: Stop it, Sitti. She's my favourite.

SITTI: Why is she dressed like that? Where's her mother?

HAYAAT: Sitti.

MAMA: Mama, it's modern. That's what they wear now.

TARIQ: Shh. Shh. They're going to announce who's eliminated.

SITTI: I never liked her.

She points to the screen.

She sounds like a *h'mar*. Eee-aw. Eee-aw.

The family laugh.

MAMA: *Ya, Mama.* Stop it. She's not a donkey. Her voice is nice. She just needs to change the songs.

SITTI: Pffft! What would you know?

TARIQ: Shh. Listen.

We hear the sound of audience response to the announcement.

Oh no! She's been eliminated.

SITTI: See? I was right. *H'mar*. Eee-aw. Eee-aw! I'm going to bed. Help me, Tariq.

MAMA *turns off the television.* TARIQ *helps* SITTI *to get up slowly.* SITTI *lets out a fart. As they exit …*

TARIQ: Ah, Sitti. I'm going to ask the Israelis for a gas mask.

SITTI: *Ya*, that Ades from last night. Oof! It always makes me windy!

TARIQ: Goodnight.

He holds his nose closed.

Wish me luck.

MAMA, BABA *and* HAYAAT *are left alone.*

MAMA: Hayaat, it's bedtime. *Yallah.*

HAYAAT: But I have to finish this homework. I have to write a poem … like the Michael Jackson song 'Do You Remember the Time', all about what I remember.

MAMA: Always about the past. Turn the lights off when you finish.

She goes to kiss HAYAAT *and cups* HAYAAT*'s face in her hands.*

Ya, Habibti. Wasted.

The face of Maysaa snaps up on the screen and down again so quickly we almost miss it.

MAMA *exits.* BABA *and* HAYAAT *exchange a look.*

BABA: Goodnight, Habibti.

BABA *kisses her on the head and exits.*

Lighting change.

HAYAAT *is writing away and begins to sing the song 'Do You Remember the Time'.*

She gets distracted by her thoughts ...

HAYAAT: [*to the audience*] I remember the time I saw my first ... well, my first and only movie at a cinema. It was in Ramallah when it was easy to travel. I ate all my popcorn and drank my Pepsi in the first ten minutes.

I remember ... when Tariq was born and Mama bit Baba's arm during a contraction and drew blood.

I remember ... the time I was voted the best Dabke dancer in my class and Maysaa was voted second best.

She catches herself.

We see Maysaa appear on the screen, dancing.

I remember ... Maysaa ... upside-down braids ... buck teeth ... her tongue sticking out when she concentrated ... I don't remember much else ...

MAMA: [*from offstage*] Hayaat! Bed!

The image of Maysaa disappears.

HAYAAT *packs her books away. She exits*

SCENE SIX: CURFEW BREAKS

Morning.

In the kitchen.

A siren indicates the evening curfew is over.

HAYAAT *is preparing for school.*

SITTI *is sitting at the table.* TARIQ *is also getting ready for school, but slowly.*

MAMA *is bustling around the kitchen and* BABA *is drinking his coffee.*

MAMA: Thank God. Move it. You'll be late.
SITTI: Make sure you drink up that knowledge, *ya Hayaat.*
HAYAAT: Yes, Sitti.
MAMA: [*quietly*] She only has education going for her now. Who will marry her with those scars?
SITTI: Don't worry, Nur. Every pea has a pod. My Hayaat is royalty, I tell you.
TARIQ: She could marry someone blind.
MAMA: Don't be *akbul*!

She clips him on the back of the head.

BABA: Go get your shoes. I'll take you to school.
SAMY: [*from offstage*] *Ya, Hayaat!*
HAYAAT: [*yelling out the window*] Coming, Samy!
MAMA: It's unnatural that she's so friendly with that boy. He's trouble.
BABA: Let her be.
MAMA: She has no girlfriends, *ya Foad.* Not since …

She indicates her face.

She hates to be around girls. She hates being around anyone except Samy. *Hada ghalat.* It's wrong.
BABA: Nur, is it not obvious why she doesn't want to be around girls?
MAMA: Well yes, but there is something wrong about *that* friendship. *That* boy. I don't like it. It frightens me. He's trouble.
BABA: Pah! They're both children, so let them enjoy their innocence while they still have it.
HAYAAT: Hello, everyone. I can hear you. I'm leaving now.
SAMY: [*from outside*] *Ya, Hayaat.* Come on!

HAYAAT *exits.*

SCENE SEVEN: ON THE WAY TO SCHOOL

Outside Hayaat's apartment.

SAMY *is waiting.* HAYAAT *enters.*

We hear the morning sounds of a busy street—honking taxis, donkey carts, minibuses.

SAMY: What took you so long? Well?

HAYAAT: Well what?

SAMY: You know what. Who's been eliminated?

HAYAAT: Samy.

SAMY: Start from the beginning.

HAYAAT: You really need to convince your aunt and uncle to buy you a television.

SAMY: Come on. Tell me.

HAYAAT: Hello, Hayaat. How are you, Hayaat? How was the last week under curfew for you, Hayaat?

SAMY: Come on. Who was eliminated?

HAYAAT: Rowetta Satchell.

SAMY: Rowetta? Oh no! No! Why? She was my favourite!

HAYAAT: Seriously, Samy, you need to get a television. Or … now that the curfew is over you can come to our apartment and watch it with us.

SAMY: Oh, yeah. And that will happen. Your mother hates me.

HAYAAT: She does not.

SAMY: She does. I see the way her eyes narrow when she looks at me on the street.

And anyway, my aunt and uncle wouldn't let me come. They believe that television is the work of the devil and music is the devil's hobby. I tell you, Hayaat, they don't get it.

Come on. I'll race you to school. I need to move again. These curfews are killing me.

SAMY *runs off.*

HAYAAT: [*to the audience*] He's right. Mama hates him. [*To* SAMY] Not so fast! Slow down!

HAYAAT *follows* SAMY *off.*

They reappear, puffed out, and stop to rest near the wall. SAMY *notices a change in the wall.*

SAMY: They're working fast. I could climb over this part of the wall last week.

HAYAAT: When do you think it will be finished?

SAMY: I don't know. Soon probably.

HAYAAT: It's cut the street in half …

SAMY *climbs up onto a tree branch to see over the wall, but it is too high.*

SAMY: It's too high now. The street sign's on the other side.

HAYAAT: This side of the street doesn't have a name now.

Beat.

I hate this wall.

SAMY: When I see it I think of Rawya and her brother Hisham. I can't believe they knocked their house down with him in it. To make way for a wall.

HAYAAT: I can't believe it.

SAMY: He wouldn't have heard them coming. He was deaf. They crushed him. Flattened … by a bulldozer.

HAYAAT: What are they doing?

An image of Maysaa appears on the wall behind HAYAAT. HAYAAT *feels Maysaa's presence but does not look at the wall. She goes very quiet.*

SAMY: The neighbours tried to stop them, but they were held back by the soldiers. Poor Rawya. She wasn't even there when it happened.

HAYAAT: Poor Maysaa.

SAMY *clocks what* HAYAAT *has just said but says nothing.*

HAYAAT *snaps herself out of her state.*

SAMY *picks up a rock and throws it at the wall in anger and the image of Maysaa disappears.*

SAMY: I told you. Adults are useless.

We hear a school bell.

Come on.

SAMY *and* HAYAAT *exit.*

SCENE EIGHT: SITTI CAN'T SLEEP

Before dawn.

SITTI *is sitting on her chair. She is holding a box with photos in it.*

HAYAAT *enters.*

HAYAAT: Why are you awake, Sitti?

SITTI: *Mish adreh anam.* Sleep wouldn't come, my darling. Your grandfather. I miss him.

HAYAAT: I wish I'd met him.

SITTI: You would have loved him, Habibti. And he would have loved you.

She sees another photo.

I miss Jerusalem, Hayaat. I try not to complain. You've all lost your home too. So I keep it inside, like your father does. *Bakalee fi albi zayoh.*

My olive trees. And my pomegranate tree. Oh, how I miss them all.

And why are you awake, Habibti?

HAYAAT: I had a bad dream. I couldn't sleep. Mama told me what happened in Beit Jala.

SITTI: Ah, Habibti. Your poor father. It was a terrible day. Just like the day I lost my home. And it continues today. It's criminal.

HAYAAT: I just don't understand. Why? How did this start?

SITTI: We were driven out.

HAYAAT: How?

SITTI: The Israelis forced us out in 1948. It never occurred to us that we wouldn't return.

HAYAAT: What did you do?

SITTI: We took what we could carry. We locked the doors, thinking we'd come back. *Tkayali hada.* We fled!

HAYAAT: To where?

SITTI: A refugee camp. The State of Israel was declared soon after and I didn't see my home again for nearly twenty years, Habibti.

HAYAAT: You must hate them, Sitti.

SITTI: Hate will not return my land to me, Hayaat. We Arabs say that the wound that bleeds inwardly is the most dangerous. *Eljoroh ily binsef fi aldakhel khatar (bijrah).* I do not hate. I simply want justice.

She rifles through her box.

Here.

HAYAAT: What is it?

SITTI: The deeds to my land and … the key to my home. We lost our friends and our family. *Masahelna nwade hum.*

HAYAAT: Did you ever try to go back, Sitti?

SITTI: We did, in 1967, after the Six Day War. Many of our homes were occupied by Jewish families. Some parts had changed so much. We walked through the village and I could hear the silence of my people. *Shabah hom kan mrafiynah.* They were like ghosts hovering around us.

HAYAAT: Was your house occupied?

SITTI: It was.

HAYAAT: Did you try to get it back?

SITTI: We tried.

HAYAAT: But … did you fight?

Images of the settlements in Jerusalem slowly fade up.

SCENE NINE: JERUSALEM

1967.

SITTI *and* SIDI *stand at the door of their home in Jerusalem. The front door opens and a* JEWISH MAN *and* WOMAN *appear. She is holding a cooking pot.*

JEWISH MAN: Get off our property!

SITTI: This is our land.

JEWISH WOMAN: No. It is our land.

SIDI *pulls the deeds out of his pocket and shows them.*

SIDI: Here is the title deed to our property.

SITTI *pulls a large rustic key from her pocket and holds it up to them.*

SITTI: And our key!

She is also trying to look past them into the house.

JEWISH MAN: They mean nothing now. You abandoned your home and the State of Israel has seized it.

SITTI: Abandoned?

SIDI: We had no choice.

SITTI: We were forced out, but we were coming back. What right do you have to be in our home?

She spots her carpet in the house behind them.

My carpet! This is my home.

JEWISH WOMAN: Please. We lost our home too, and our family. My mother, my father, my brother, all gone.

SITTI: I'm sorry for what happened to your family, but this has been our home for many generations. Why must we be forced out to live in a refugee camp? Why must we be punished?

JEWISH MAN: The past is the past. The State of Israel has been declared.

SIDI: These are our papers! This is our land.

JEWISH MAN: Go to Egypt or Jordan or Syria. You have many countries from which to choose.

SITTI: Would you ask an Englishman to move to America because they speak English? Palestine is our home. Not Egypt. Not Jordan! And you're standing on my carpet and eating from my plates!

The door slams.

A lighting change snaps.

The Jerusalem images go off.

SCENE TEN: SITTI CAN'T SLEEP (PART 2)

SITTI: I was pathetic, *ya Hayaat*. In my terror, I screamed like a child. I wrapped my arms around my pomegranate tree and wouldn't let go. Your grandfather had to carry me away.

Ya, Habibti, hawalnah bus ma el assaf ma—idrah. Our fate was sealed.

I was in the refugee camp when I heard their Prime Minister Golda Meir say there were no such things as Palestinians. *La wujood lahum.* They did not exist. Her words poisoned me, Hayaat. I existed! *Ana mawjoudeh.* I exist!

If I could have one wish, it would be to touch the soil of my home one last time before I die. Land, Hayaat. There is nothing so important. I want to die on my land.

HAYAAT *takes the key from* SITTI.

I kept it all this time. And then your grandfather died.
HAYAAT: Is that when you moved in with Mama?
SITTI: Yes. She married your father and I was so happy, Hayaat. Your father had land, his olive grove and a nice big laugh.
HAYAAT: Laugh? I never hear it anymore.
SITTI: Not so surprising, Hayaat.

She puts all her things back into the box.

They do not have two heads and ten feet, Hayaat.
HAYAAT: Who? The refugees?
SITTI: No, the Jews. That woman who took my home must have kissed and played with her children. Like me, she knew pain and suffering and torment of losing one's family and home.
HAYAAT: Do you think they laugh?
SITTI: Of course they laugh. It is just that nobody has realised that laughter sounds the same whether it shakes its way out of a Jew or an Arab.
HAYAAT: But it's wrong, Sitti. It's so wrong. How can you accept it?
SITTI: I don't accept it, Hayaat. I've never accepted it. But we do not have the luxury to despair, Habibti. So we live.

SCENE ELEVEN: SITTI COLLAPSES

Early morning.

SITTI *is in the kitchen. She is not well and is struggling to stay up. She reaches for the coffee pot and collapses.*

MAMA: [*offstage*] Tariq! Get your bag. You'll be late for school.

HAYAAT *come into the kitchen with her bag. She discovers* SITTI *collapsing.*

HAYAAT: Sitti! Mama! Help!

MAMA *runs into the kitchen.*

Sitti, wake up! Please wake up.
MAMA: Foad! Foad! Mama has collapsed! Call the ambulance. Hayaat, get off her.

TARIQ *enters and begins to wail.*

TARIQ: Sitti! Sitti!

HAYAAT: Please. Please. Please.

TARIQ: Is she dead?

MAMA: She's collapsed. It could be her heart. Hold her head.

The children both wail and cry.

BABA *rushes in.*

BABA: The ambulance is on its way. Calm down. Take your brother to your room.

HAYAAT: No! I'm not leaving her.

BABA: She'll be fine.

HAYAAT: What if she dies?

BABA: I told you, the ambulance is on its way.

TARIQ: But what if they don't let it through the checkpoint?

BABA: We can only pray, Habibti.

MAMA: At least there is no curfew. God favours her. She is one of God's loved ones—and I was so short-tempered with her yesterday. God forgive me. I hope they get here quickly.

HAYAAT: Sitti! Sitti! Don't die. Please! Please.

BABA: Get off her, Hayaat!

HAYAAT: Stay alive, Sitti. Stay alive.

BABA *forces* HAYAAT *off* SITTI.

I'll let you touch that soil again. I promise.

An ambulance siren approaches.

MAMA: Thank God. Hayaat! We're going to go with her. Look after your brother. Don't leave the house except for school.

MAMA *exits hurriedly, leaving* HAYAAT *alone.*

HAYAAT: [*to the audience*] She can't die.

Pause.

Samy. I need Samy.

SCENE TWELVE: THE JOURNEY BEGINS

Early morning.

Outside the apartment on the way to the bus stop.

HAYAAT: Have you got everything? I've got some sandwiches and I brought some money for the bus … Oh, and my birth certificate.

SAMY: Will she be alright?

HAYAAT: I don't know. Mama said her heart is weak. Have you got everything?

SAMY: I think so.

HAYAAT: Birth certificate?

SAMY: Yes. And I stole some money from Amto Christina's charity tin. Helping Sitti Zeynab counts as charity, right?

Beat.

So what will we put the soil in?

HAYAAT: This. I've got three.

HAYAAT *pulls out an empty hummus jar from her backpack to show* SAMY.

SAMY: Good. Good. And how will we get into Jerusalem?

HAYAAT: It's only about ten kilometres away.

SAMY: But we're not allowed in, Hayaat. Remember?

HAYAAT: Come on, Samy.

SAMY: We'll never make it, Hayaat.

HAYAAT: Please. I have to save her.

SAMY: But it's impossible.

HAYAAT *looks dejected and* SAMY *notices.*

Of course, we could cut through the back roads.

HAYAAT: Really?

SAMY: We'll find people who have been turned away at the checkpoints and are taking the back roads. People do it all the time … don't they?

HAYAAT: I think.

SAMY: We'll need to take a bus. I'm sure we'll manage. There must be a way to sneak in.

HAYAAT: What if we die?

Beat.

SAMY: I probably won't. I have my cross for protection. I can lend you one if you like. But you're Muslim so it might not work.

HAYAAT: Yeah, probably not.

SAMY: Anyway, you'll be a martyr.

HAYAAT: I'd rather live.

SAMY; Yeah, me too. And I have to be back before dark because Amo Joseph is forcing me to go to church tonight. A special mass.

HAYAAT: Is it as boring as prayers at the mosque?

SAMY: It numbs my brain. My uncle can see I pay no attention and clips me over the ears every two minutes. I'm actually grateful. At least it keeps me awake.

HAYAAT: I close my eyes during prayers, and when Mama accuses me of lacking faith, I tell her that closing my eyes brings me closer to Allah. She beams.

Pause.

SAMY: You know, Father Anthony is always preaching to us about being strong in the face of oppression. Never give in or be a coward against the occupation. Then I see him forced to strip down to his underpants at a checkpoint the other day. All the soldiers laughing at him. Where was his courage? Adults are no use, Hayaat. They can't protect us or themselves.

HAYAAT: [*to the audience*] Samy was six when he saw his father being dragged out of the house by the Israeli Internal Security Service. They beat him up and took him. I think his mum died of a heart attack after that. We moved to Bethlehem when I was nine so I never knew his parents.

SCENE THIRTEEN: WASIM

Early morning.

At the bus stop. The sun is already hot.

WASIM, *a young boy the same age as* HAYAAT *and* SAMY, *enters. He is scruffy and is clearly from the refugee settlement. He is selling tissues.*

WASIM: Tissues? Tissues? May God give you a long life.

SAMY: Go away, kid. Do we look like tourists to you? We're waiting for a bus. We've got important business.

WASIM: What business do you have?

SAMY: We're on a private mission.
WASIM: Tell me.
HAYAAT: Where are you from?
WASIM: I'm from the Aida refugee camp. Are you from there too?
HAYAAT: Certainly not!
WASIM: Tell me about your mission.
HAYAAT: Go away. We don't have time for you.
WASIM: Why is your face like that? What happened to you? Does it hurt?
HAYAAT: Shut up. Leave me alone, you filthy, stinking refugee! Why don't you wash? Your clothes are filthy. They smell.
SAMY: Yeah.

WASIM*'s eyes moisten, but he tries to hide it.* HAYAAT *feels very guilty and pulls out some money.*

HAYAAT: I'll take the whole lot.
WASIM: What?
HAYAAT: The tissues. Give me the lot.

WASIM *gives her all his tissues and* HAYAAT *pays him.*

SAMY: What are we going to do with all of those?
HAYAAT: What we do with them isn't the point.
WASIM: I'm Wasim
HAYAAT: I'm Hayaat.
SAMY: Samy.
WASIM: Do you play soccer?
SAMY: Yes. You?
WASIM: I'm on the United Nations sponsored soccer team.
SAMY: What? How did you get picked? You're a refugee kid.
WASIM: That's why they took pity on me. I'm going to be properly trained. With proper soccer boots, and T-shirt and knee pads.
SAMY: Knee pads? Huh. Liar.
WASIM: I swear to God, *ya zalami*. And the trainer is from England with a proper accent and everything.
SAMY: Stop lying.
WASIM: I promise on my mother's grave. They came to the camp to help the kids, saw we loved soccer, and they sponsored a team. Do you want to practise with me? We could do it every week.
HAYAAT: Where will you play?

WASIM: In Italy.

SAMY *is distressed by this new information.*

SAMY: Italy? Really? Well, can't … can't you ask the coach to let me play too? I'm excellent. Hayaat, tell him how excellent I am. Tell him!

HAYAAT: He's terrible.

SAMY: Hayaat!

HAYAAT: I'm only joking. He's really, really good.

WASIM: Okay. I'll see what I can do.

SAMY: So you'll ask the coach?

WASIM: Maybe we can play together for a while and then I can ask him.

HAYAAT: Come on, Samy. We need to find out how to get to Jerusalem.

WASIM: I can tell you.

HAYAAT: How would you know?

WASIM: My father goes there for work.

SAMY: How does he get in? Does he have a green pass?

WASIM: No. He travels across the mountains and sleeps in the caves.

HAYAAT: Is there another way?

WASIM *picks up a stick and draws a map on the ground.*

WASIM: Well … The ordinary way from Bethlehem to Jerusalem is to first go to Beit Jala.

Then you go direct to Jerusalem from there. This way should only take twenty minutes, depending on what sort of identity card you've got. If your parents have a blue one then you're an Israeli and you can go this way. If you have a green one, then you're a West Banker. I bet you're both green like me.

They nod.

Well then, you're crazy people. *Majneen*. It's forbidden for you to go that way. You'll have to go another way. It's full of risks and it's a lot longer.

So … you'll have to go from Bethlehem to Beit Sahur to Deir Salah then to al'Obadiah.

HAYAAT: Oof! How long will that take?

WASIM *continues with his stick and map.*

WASIM: Bethlehem to Beit Sahur is twenty minutes on foot and five or six by car.

Beit Sahur to Deir Salah is a forty-minute journey on foot and ten by car. From Deir Salah to al'Obadiah about ten minutes by foot or two by car. One of you should be adding these figures together … And then after that you have to pass the valley …

SAMY: Wadi Al-Nar?

HAYAAT: Valley of Fire? I hate it. It's all windy and narrow—full of rocks and sand. We had to drive through there on the way to Ramallah once. It made me sick.

WASIM: It's the only way, so there's no point complaining.

Anyway, after you pass this valley you go through Al Sawahreh then Abo Dees and finally El Eizarya.

Just after El Eizarya, you'll find a checkpoint before you enter the Old City in Jerusalem and a soldier will inspect your papers.

But … because you're from the West Bank you'll never be allowed through. And that's that.

But those are just the details.

The sound of a bus arriving.

Here's the bus … Go. I'll see you when you come back. And we can start practising. I would come with you but my father will kill me.

SCENE FOURTEEN: ON THE BUS TO BEIT SAHUR

We cut to the bus en route. The bus shakes and jolts as it makes its way.

The driver is ABO AZAM *and there is a female passenger seated. She is* AMTO AMAL.

The manner of ABO AZAM*'s driving is indicated by the passengers' faces—tense. He is driving fast and swerving everywhere.*

At one point he almost hits a man and donkey on the road. He swerves. The passengers scream.

ABO AZAM: What a close one, eh?

SAMY: Close one?! You nearly killed that poor donkey!

The bus drives on. Silence.

Do you think Sitti will be alright?

HAYAAT: I really don't know, Samy. Her heart is weak and she's old.

The woman, AMTO AMAL, *looks over her shoulder at them.*

AMTO AMAL: Aren't you Nur's daughter?

HAYAAT *freezes.*

Yes. Yes. I know your face. It was ruined by them. And your friend, what was her name? Tragic. I'm Amto Amal. Do you remember me? Your mother and I used to volunteer at the Arab Women's Union. What are you doing on this bus? And *who* is this boy with you?

SAMY: Don't listen to her.

AMTO AMAL: He's not your brother. [*To the other passengers*] Her brother is much younger. [*Back to the girls*] Where are you both going?

HAYAAT: Nowhere.

AMTO AMAL: Passengers on a bus do not go *no*where! Why are you on this service alone?

HAYAAT: Um … er … mmm …

ABO AZAM: Leave them be, *ya ekhti*. You're going to make her cry.

AMTO AMAL: *Ya khayi*. They are children on a bus through Wadi al-Nar. Why are you alone? Your mother would be sick with worry if she had any idea.

SAMY: It's our business.

AMTO AMAL: *Shur*. Didn't your parents teach you any manners, *ya walad*?

SAMY: They taught me to mind my own business.

HAYAAT: Samy.

AMTO AMAL *reaches for her phone. She is looking for Hayaat's mother's number.*

ABO AZAM: Another passenger.

The bus comes to a screeching halt.

The door opens.

SAMY *looks at* HAYAAT. *They both grab their bags.*

SAMY: Let's go. Run.

As the doors open, HAYAAT *and* SAMY *escape.*

The door closes.

AMTO AMAL: Bus driver, stop! Don't let them get away! We must do something! Stop them!

The bus drives away and we see AMTO AMAL *on the phone.* SAMY *waves at her makes a rude gesture. He is angry.*

HAYAAT: Samy, stop. She's calling my mum. It's bad enough as it is.

SCENE FIFTEEN: BETWEEN BEIT SAHUR AND DEIR SALAH

SAMY *and* HAYAAT *are in a field surrounded by mountains. The view is breathtaking.*

HAYAAT: Now what?

SAMY *doesn't respond.*

Okay … well … we've passed Beit Sahur so we must be close to Deir Salah. Wasim said it was about forty minutes away. We can catch another bus when we get there. Let's just walk.

As they walk, HAYAAT *picks up stones and rocks along the way and examines them.* SAMY *walks ahead silently.*

Hello. You're quiet.

SAMY: In a fortnight, it will be seven years …

Pause.

HAYAAT: How long since you saw him?

SAMY: Three years.

HAYAAT: Why so long?

SAMY: We're not allowed to visit anymore.

HAYAAT: I think your father's a hero, Samy.

SAMY *ignores the comment.*

Do you write?

SAMY: Sometimes.

Silence.

HAYAAT: You should send him photos.

SAMY: We do. Amto Christina sends them.

HAYAAT: Does he write back?

SAMY: Sometimes.

HAYAAT: He's a hero. Locked up all these years for no reason other than organising protests and strikes.

SAMY: He traded me for the cause, Hayaat!

Silence.

Just imagine. Italy … a real soccer team. This is my chance.

SCENE SIXTEEN: ON THE BUS IN DEIR SALAH

A bus stop, Deir Salah.

The bus arrives. HAYAAT *and* SAMY *join the bus driver* KARIM.

SAMY: How far is it to Jerusalem?

KARIM: Forty-five minutes. Maybe one hour. Unless the Israelis have other plans. One can never be certain these days. I'm Karim. Take a seat.

MOLLY *boards the bus. She is covered in two shawls, one is Palestinian and the other is Israeli.*

She greets KARIM.

MOLLY: Shalom.

KARIM: *W'laikum. Salam.* Welcome aboard.

SAMY *and* HAYAAT *are stunned at the two shawls.*

SAMY: Why are you letting her on board? She's an Israeli. She's wearing both shawls, Karim.

KARIM: I don't care if she prays in a synagogue or shaves her hair for Buddha. Anybody who pays their fare is welcome on my service.

KARIM *starts the bus and they begin to travel.*

Silence.

SAMY *points to the Palestinian shawl.*

SAMY: [*to* MOLLY] What do you mean wearing our shawl?

MOLLY: I'm against the occupation.

SAMY: Really? You're still an Israeli.

MOLLY: True. And you're a Palestinian. What of it?

SAMY: So why don't you take the Israeli only bypass road? It's much quicker.

MOLLY: I'm a peace activist. I'm on checkpoint watch.

She indicates her camera.

We keep an eye out. We make sure people pass through safely. It's better that we travel this way.

Beat. MOLLY *looks at* HAYAAT *and* SAMY.

You're travelling alone?

SAMY: So?

MOLLY: It's strange, that's all. And dangerous.

Everything goes quiet for a while.

KARIM *turns the radio on and Kazem al Saher comes on the radio, spouting poetry.*

HAYAAT: Oh no, it's Kazem al Saher. He sings poetry!

Time passes.

KARIM: We're passing ol-Obadiah.

The passengers all look out the window.

SAMY: [*to* HAYAAT] She's probably an Israeli agent.

HAYAAT: *Samy!*

SAMY: [*to* MOLLY] Where do you come from?

MOLLY: Tel Aviv. But I've been an American citizen for ten years now.

KARIM: So what's your story then? The majority of Israelis I see on this route have guns in their hands.

MOLLY: I'm working with a human rights watch group. We send photos. We tell stories. To make sure the world knows. Not everyone supports what's happening.

SAMY: What a joke.

MOLLY: I've paid my price for my beliefs. I was forced to leave my birthplace even though I was part of the IDF.

HAYAAT: The IDF? You were part of the army?

MOLLY: Conscription is compulsory.

SAMY: You're occupying our land!

MOLLY: Yes, we are. I can't accept it either. We need to share this land as equals.

SAMY: Tell your government. Tell the settlers who sit on the tops of our mountains, watching us like we're cockroaches.

MOLLY: I don't have all the answers. I just know that this can't go on. The occupation steals from the occupier and the occupied. We are all losers. It's a mess.

KARIM: Well, here's another mess. Sorry, my friends. We have to stop. They've put in a flying checkpoint along the way today. Let us hope our Israeli friend here is our Messiah.

MOLLY: I'm not the Messiah, Karim. I'm a Jew against the occupation. I don't expect any sympathy from the soldiers. But I do have my camera. It's a powerful weapon!

KARIM *pulls the bus over to the side of the road.*

SCENE SEVENTEEN: FLYING CHECKPOINT

The lighting snaps to outside the bus.

SOLDIER: Everybody out! Line up. Passes ready!

SAMY: *H'mar!*

HAYAAT: Samy. Don't!

SAMY *and* HAYAAT *begin fumbling in their bags for their identification.*

The SOLDIER *first looks at* KARIM*'s then* MOLLY*'s, then* SAMY*'s identification. The* SOLDIER *moves slowly.*

HAYAAT *is very nervous and drops her birth certificate.*

SOLDIER: Pick it up!

HAYAAT *picks it up and nervously hands it to him.*

You nervous? You've got something to hide?

HAYAAT: No … nothing to hide.

SOLDIER: Where are you going?

SAMY: We're going to Abo Dees to visit fam—

SOLDIER: Did I ask you?

Silence.

The SOLDIER *points his gun at* HAYAAT*'s face and indicates for her to step aside from the group.*

Where are you going?

HAYAAT. To visit family.

SOLDIER: Where?

HAYAAT: Abo Dees.

The SOLDIER *circles around* HAYAAT, *paying close attention to her face. He walks away.*

The following conversation is in Hebrew and English.

MOLLY: What are you doing? Why is this road closed?

SOLDIER: Because it is.

MOLLY: But we're all trying to go about our business.

SOLDIER: The road is closed.

MOLLY: This is pathetic and you know it. These are innocent people.

SOLDIER: The road is closed.

MOLLY: But what about the bus? Can it pass?

SOLDIER: No bus. You have to walk.

MOLLY *returns to the group.*

MOLLY: It's no good. We have to walk.

HAYAAT: To where?

MOLLY: To the Container Checkpoint.

SAMY: That makes no sense.

KARIM: What does sense have to do with it?

MOLLY: [*to* KARIM] I'm sorry. I tried, Karim. I'm sorry. The bus isn't allowed to go through. You have to return to Bethlehem.

KARIM *collects his things. He jumps back on his bus.*

SAMY: So why are some buses allowed through and others aren't?

MOLLY: Who knows. Maybe they don't like Karim's face.

KARIM: I knew it. My good looks are a security threat. I tell my wife but she doesn't believe me.

MOLLY: We'll have to walk on and catch one of the buses that are allowed to pass through.

HAYAAT: We'll never get there.

KARIM: Trust in Allah, my little sister. Trust in Allah.

KARIM *drives away.*

SCENE EIGHTEEN: WALKING TO THE CHECKPOINT AND THE NEXT BUS

MOLLY, SAMY *and* HAYAAT *walk towards the checkpoint.*

MOLLY: So you have family in Abo Dees.

SAMY *and* HAYAAT *exchange a look.*

Where are you really going?

HAYAAT: To Jerusalem. To my grandmother's village. She hasn't been there since 1967. I need to go for her.

MOLLY: You do have the papers to enter, right?

SAMY: *Bin kalb* to the papers. We'll get in.

MOLLY: What? Are you kids crazy? You realise that it's dangerous? What do you need so badly that's worth risking your life for?

SAMY: Her grandmother's dying.

MOLLY: Well, you could die. I don't think you understand. You can't get in without the correct papers.

HAYAAT: I need to get soil. For Sitti Zeynab.

SAMY: I've got an idea. Give me a jar. We'll fill a jar from each part of the journey. We'll fill one with the soil of Wadi al Nar. One from the checkpoint into Jerusalem and one with the soil from your grandmother's village.

MOLLY: You are risking your life for a bit of dirt?

SAMY: And that is the difference between your people and us.

They walk.

Lighting change.

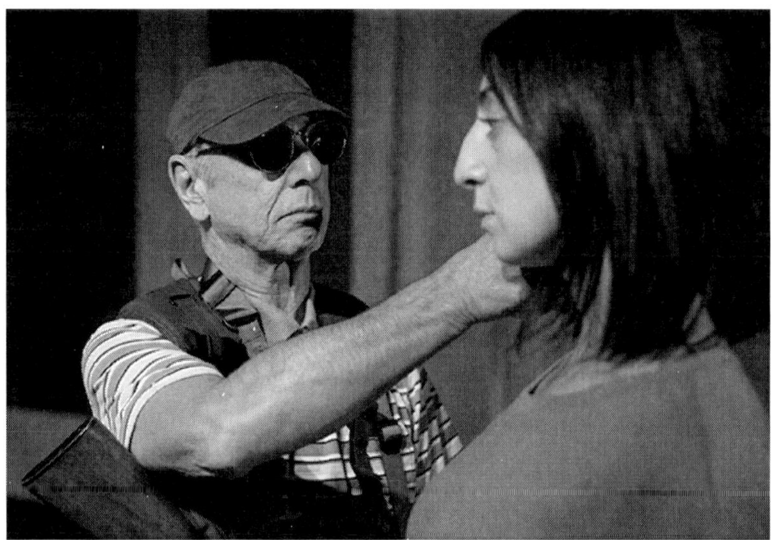

Sal Sharah (left) as a soldier and Aanisa Vylet as Hayaat in the 2017 Monkey Baa production at Lendlease Darling Quarter Theatre, Sydney. (Photo: Michael Bourchier)

On the bus to the Container Checkpoint.

They are all standing in this bus as it is very full. They are packed like sardines.

As it drives along, they all look out the window.

HAYAAT *spots three blindfolded men kneeling on the roadside with soldiers beside them.*

She touches SAMY *on the arm.*

They both look.

MOLLY *sees the same thing and takes a photo of the men.*

We see the photo flashed up on the screen.

This action is repeated with other scenarios.

An old couple at the boot of their car which is full of gifts.

Children on their own. Then ...

A whole panoramic view of Jerusalem appears on the screen.

HAYAAT: Oh, Jerusalem.

SAMY: We're nearly there, Hayaat.

They finally arrive at the Container Checkpoint and the bus stops.

Photos are flashed up on the screen of different angles of the checkpoint and the people waiting.

A SOLDIER *appears at the bus.*

SOLDIER: Everybody out! Papers!

The passengers all exit the bus and pull out their papers.

The SOLDIER *pulls* HAYAAT *and* SAMY *aside.* MOLLY *tries to follow but the* SOLDIER *stops her.* MOLLY *pulls out her camera.*

And why are you travelling without your parents?

SAMY: Because you killed one and imprisoned the other.

HAYAAT: Samy!

SOLDIER: So. You're the son of a prisoner. Not thinking of being a terrorist like your father I hope.

SAMY: He's a hero.

The SOLDIER *grabs the jar from* HAYAAT.

SOLDIER: And what is this?
SAMY: Palestine.
SOLDIER: Palestine. There's your Palestine.

The SOLDIER *smashes the jar to pieces.*

She points her gun at SAMY *and* HAYAAT. MOLLY *joins them with her camera. The* SOLDIER *walks away laughing. She waves the bus away without them.* SAMY *is very angry.* HAYAAT *drags him away.*

HAYAAT: Samy, please. Stay calm. We've got more jars. We'll get more soil. Please.
MOLLY: Calm down. Calm down. It's okay.

SAMY *is silent.* HAYAAT *nods.*

HAYAAT, MOLLY *and* SAMY *walk towards the looming wall.*

That section's gone up fast. Wasn't here two months ago.
HAYAAT: Now what do we do? We'll never make it. Can we find another bus?
SAMY: Look. That part of the wall isn't finished. It's not that high. We could climb over it.
MOLLY: No. It's too dangerous. You don't know what's on the other side.
HAYAAT: Molly's right, Samy.
MOLLY: It's just too dangerous, Samy.
SAMY: Hayaat, we've come this far. We can't go back.
MOLLY: I can't let you go over.

There is a moment of pause in SAMY *and* HAYAAT *and then ...*

SAMY: Run, Hayaat!
MOLLY: Samy, no! Hayaat!

HAYAAT *and* SAMY *run.*

No!

SCENE NINETEEN: OVER THE WALL

SAMY *and* HAYAAT *run a distance once they land on the other side of the wall and finally throw themselves on the ground, exhausted.*

HAYAAT: We made it, Samy. We made it! Jerusalem!

SAMY *kisses his cross.*

SAMY: I always knew we would.

They dance the Dabke in celebration.

Give me a jar. Jerusalem soil.

HAYAAT *hands* SAMY *a jar from her bag.* SAMY *fills the jar with soil.*

HAYAAT: Come on. We need to find out how to get to the Old City.

They go to move and are startled by the whistle from a man leaning up against the wall. YOSSI. *He is thin and short. He is mid-forties. He is wearing a white shirt and tie and when he lifts his arms he has large yellow sweat stains under his arms.*

YOSSI: *Shalom.*

SAMY: Stay calm, Hayaat. [*To* YOSSI] *Salam.* How far is it to the Old City?

YOSSI: The Old City, hey?

SAMY: Yes. How far is it? My sister and I are trying to find our way to a private hospital in West Jerusalem. We want to see our aunt before she dies.

YOSSI: Must be a close aunt, yes?

SAMY: Very close. She raised us. Isn't that right, Hayaat?

HAYAAT: Yes. Very close.

YOSSI: And you have passes?

SAMY: Um … is it possible … to um …?

YOSSI: Come on, kids.

HAYAAT: Please. Okay, we lied … but we really need to get there. See my face? I have to find a specialist … and we don't have passes.

YOSSI *acknowledges* HAYAAT*'s scars.*

YOSSI: I can help you.

HAYAAT: Are you sure?

YOSSI: My friends and I do this all the time. We smuggle people into West Jerusalem in our cars.

HAYAAT: Have you ever been caught?

YOSSI: I've got yellow number plates. I get through. It will be fine.

HAYAAT *becomes worried all of a sudden. She pulls* SAMY *aside.*

Maysaa appears faintly on the screen behind them.

SAMY *puts his arm around* HAYAAT.

SAMY: For Sitti Zeynab.

Maysaa fades.

HAYAAT *returns to* YOSSI *and hands over the money.*

HAYAAT: Thank you.

YOSSI: Get your papers and put them in your pockets. Lie down on the floor. Throw this blanket over you. No-one will notice.

Are you settled?

Two muffled 'yes' sounds come from under the blanket.

Don't talk.

The taxi departs. They drive quietly for a while.

We see an image of the Damascus Gate.

We just passed the Damascus Gate.

Muffled 'yay's come from under the blanket.

They drive a little while longer.

The wailing sirens of police cars.

The taxi stops.

I can't believe it.

SAMY: What?

HAYAAT: Have we been caught?

YOSSI: A protest. Of all days. The road's blocked.

HAYAAT: What do we do?

YOSSI: It's too dangerous to stay in here. You have to get out quickly. Lose yourselves in the crowd. Are you ready? Go! Now! Before you get stuck here! Quick! God be with you!

Go!

SAMY *and* HAYAAT *rush out into the protest.*

SAMY: [*to* HAYAAT] Don't lose me. Stay close!

They are in a crowd of protestors, surrounded by military jeeps, police cars and soldiers.

We can hear chanting. It gets louder. There are placards and Palestinian flags being waved.

It is mayhem. SAMY *and* HAYAAT *become separated.*

HAYAAT: Samy! Samy! Samy! The soil for Sitti. I need to get the soil for Sitti.

The hissing sound from teargas.

The protest is surrounded in gas.

People are shouting and crying.

HAYAAT *falls to her knees.*

We hear people running and calling out. 'Run! Run! They're coming!' A crescendo of sounds.

SCENE TWENTY: MAYSAA VISITS

Lighting change.

HAYAAT: 'We need to join the protest', Maysaa says to me. 'We need to let the soldiers know we won't be silenced. The more voices the better, Hayaat', she says. I agree.

The soldiers are demolishing the home of a man as punishment for his links to a suicide bomber. The man's been shot. His family's home is being destroyed as a warning to all.

We stand with the dead man's family, singing loudly in protest.

The bulldozers attack.

'I can't bear to look', Maysaa says.

The women wail.

The walls, the pipes, the kitchen cupboards, smashed. The house collapses.

There's nothing we can do.

The bulldozers keep going.

'Let's just leave', says Maysaa. 'We need to get out. Quick!'

The soldiers fire their guns to scatter us. The single shots whistle past, lodging into walls of houses behind us, smashing into windows of parked cars. Volleys of shots explode in the air.

People scream, others pick up stones and throw them at the soldiers. It's all we have.

Jeeps are chasing the crowd. The soldiers shoot in all directions.

'Run!' people cry. We run with the other kids.

We try to find a building or an alleyway to hide in.

In our panic Maysaa and I trip over each other. '*Yallah*. Quick, Maysaa!'

We try to stand up. See the jeep stop at the end of the alley. We're trapped. The soldier pushes the barrel of his rifle through an opening in the front window and …

A gunshot rings out.

Excruciating pain. I want Mama. I turn to grab Maysaa. She's crumpled on the ground. I kneel down beside her. My face oozing blood. I hold my hand up to my bleeding face, look at Maysaa, and vomit.

She died with her eyes open.

SCENE TWENTY-ONE: BACK FROM JERUSALEM

It is evening.

HAYAAT *enters with her backpack which holds the jar of soil from Jerusalem.*

HAYAAT: Sitti.

SITTI: Hayaat!

HAYAAT: Sitti! You're okay.

SITTI: Oh, how happy I am to see you. I was so worried about you. Do me a favour, Habibti. Don't let your mother feed me any more of her soup. Tell me, Hayaat. Where have you been?

HAYAAT: I was so scared, Sitti. Ever since the day Maysaa died. She's been wrapped around my neck. And then when we were in Jerusalem—

SITTI: Jerusalem?

HAYAAT: Yes. We made it. But we got caught in a protest and … That's when I remembered everything. I feel so guilty because she died … But I can't help think about my face … I'm so weak.

SITTI: Your soul is strong, Hayaat. Ignore the fat aunties and uncles who pity you because of your scars. I don't pity you. I look up to you. But, why would you enter Jerusalem?

HAYAAT: I tried, Sitti. I really tried to reach your village. To bring you back some soil.

SITTI: *Ya Allah!* Habibti! You went because of me?

HAYAAT: Yes.

She unzips her bag and pulls out a hummus jar.

SITTI *can't work it out.*

Open your hands.

SITTI *holds open her palms and* HAYAAT *pours some soil into them.*

Jerusalem soil.

Silence.

SITTI: Habibti.

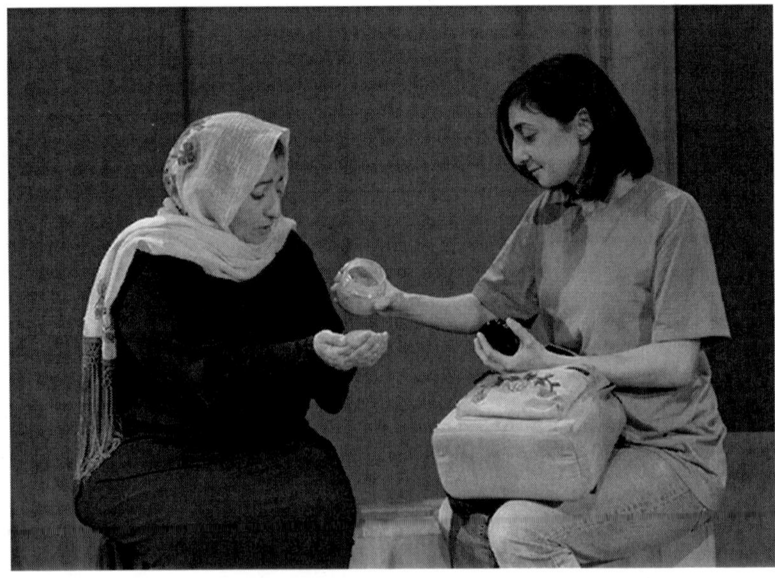

Alissar Gazal (left) as Sitti Zeynab and Aanisa Vylet as Hayaat in the 2017 Monkey Baa production at Lendlease Darling Quarter Theatre, Sydney. (Photo: Michael Bourchier)

SCENE TWENTY-TWO: THE AIDA CAMP

WASIM *is waiting with his soccer ball.* SAMY *enters excited.* HAYAAT *is with him.*

WASIM: I waited at the pharmacy this week, *ya zalami*. We were going to play soccer.
SAMY: Did you speak to the coach?
WASIM: What coach?

He remembers his lie and tries to make light of it.

You knew that wasn't true, *ya zalami*. We can still play soccer, can't we?
SAMY: You swore you were telling the truth. On your mother's grave.
WASIM: My mother's not dead.
SAMY: I believed you. Soccer boots. Knee pads. Italy!
HAYAAT: Why did you lie, Wasim?
WASIM: I don't know.
SAMY: You're all talk! Just like the rest of them! Talk talk talk!

SAMY *lunges at* WASIM.

WASIM: I'm sorry.
SAMY: You made me believe I could get out of this hell hole. You liar!
WASIM: I said I'm sorry!
HAYAAT: Get off him, Samy!
SAMY: I'm going to beat the hell out of you.
HAYAAT: No!
SAMY: Stay out of this, Hayaat!
WASIM: Get off me!
HAYAAT: Samy, stop! Have you gone mad?!
WASIM: Don't hurt me!
SAMY: You lied to me!
WASIM: No!

WASIM *cries.*

SAMY: Go! Go! Go!

WASIM *runs off.*

HAYAAT: Wait! Stop! You're acting like someone who's in a *mustashfa el-majaneen*. You're crazy.

SAMY: Mind your own business. You're always in my face.

HAYAAT: You just tried to bash Wasim, Samy!

SAMY: This has nothing to do with you! Get out of my way or I'll bash you too!

HAYAAT: Come on then! Bash me! Come on, you *h'mar*. Look at my face! There's glass lodged in there that can't be removed. You think I'm scared of you? Go ahead! Bash me!

We don't know which direction SAMY *is going to go. He is on the edge. He then screams and throws the rock against a wall.*

SAMY: If you tell anyone I cried …

HAYAAT: I didn't see you cry.

Silence.

SAMY: I told you there's no point in dreaming.

HAYAAT: It's all we have. Sitti says …

SAMY: You've got a grandmother to talk to. I can't speak to my 'Jesus this and Jesus that' aunt and uncle. They're useless. Soccer was my only chance.

HAYAAT: Samy, we can't think like that. We can't. Sitti says we don't have the luxury to despair. We've got to fight. We can't give in, Samy. We have to survive.

SAMY: I don't want to simply survive, Hayaat.

HAYAAT: Maybe it's about living with hope and purpose.

SAMY: Well, what's my purpose?

HAYAAT: How am I supposed to know?

SAMY: You said it.

HAYAAT: Well, I don't know.

SCENE TWENTY-THREE: VISITING MAYSAA

A graveyard.

BABA *and* HAYAAT *make their way to Maysaa's grave. It is* HAYAAT*'s first time at the graveyard.*

BABA: Here she is.

HAYAAT *buries her head into* BABA*'s shoulder.*

HAYAAT: She wasn't ready to leave.

BABA: She is at peace, now. And you're okay.

HAYAAT: But I wasn't, Baba. I threw all the memories of what happened that day into the ground. I buried them with Maysaa. But all the good memories got buried too.

BABA: Hayaat, you're strong. You're stronger than I am. I've failed you all.

HAYAAT: You haven't, Baba. We're here. You have us. Me and Mama and Tariq and Sitti.

BABA *prays.*

[*To the audience*] I am thirteen years old. I know the smell of a corpse. I know the sound of people screaming in terror.

The wall will be finished soon. Parts of Bethlehem will be fully deserted. Houses abandoned, schools emptied, more streets without names.

But I won't live in despair. I'll learn to love the mirror. I'll do more than survive.

We Palestinians simply want to live as a free people, with hope, and dignity and purpose.

That's all.

BABA: Are you ready to say goodbye to Maysaa?

HAYAAT: No. Never.

Blackout.

THE END